Norman Buller

Sleeping with Icons

*To my dear wife Ursula
whose unfailing love and support
made many of these poems possible*

First published in 2007
by Waterloo Press (Hove)
126 Furze Croft
Furze Hill
Hove BN3 1PF

Printed in Palatino 11pt by
One Digital
54 Hollingdean Road
East Sussex BN2 4AA

© Noman Buller 2007
All rights remain with the author.

Cover design © Alan Morrison 2007.

Norman Buller is hereby identified as author of this work in accordance with Section 77 of the Copyright, Designs and Patents Act 1988

This book is sold subject to the condition that it shall not, by way of trade of otherwise, be lent, resold, hired out or otherwise circulated without the author's prior consent in any form of binding or cover other than that in which it is published and without a similar condition including this condition being imposed on the subsequent purchaser.

A CIP record for this book is available from the British Library

ISBN 1-902731-38-7

By the same author

Thirteen Poems (Festival Pamphlets, Queen's University Belfast, 1965)
Travelling Light – Waterloo Sampler No. 12 (Waterloo Press, 2005)

Acknowledgements

Thanks go to the editors of the following journals in which some of my poetry has previously appeared: *Acumen, Agenda, California Quarterly* (US), *Cambridge Left, Chance, Chequer, Clare Market Review, Comstock Review* (US), *Communique* (S.Africa), *Concern, Envoi, Gravesiana, Interpreter's House, London Magazine, Orbis, Other Poetry, Outposts, Poetry From Cambridge, Poetry Life, Poetry News, Poetry Nottingham, The Rialto, Thames.*

Poetry Life prize, second place; the Bedford Poetry Prize, third place; the Ware Poetry Competition, first place.

Contents

Out Of the Pool

The Kiss	19
Poor Fisherman	20
Mostar	21
Francis Bacon's Pope	22
Bus Riders	23
Youth	24
Incomplete	25
Broken Kings	26
Sleeping with Icons	28
Peasants Sowing Beans	29
The Seine at Marly	30
Poets – Man and Wife	31
Observations	32

Persons Places Dreams

D.H.Lawrence	35
The Guest	36
Bavarian Cemetery	37
Renewal	38
Sir Gawayn's Lament	39
Thomas Hardy	40
Nightmare	42
Polruan	43
My Father	44
My Mother	45
Sketches from Ireland	46
The Other	47
Frankenheim	48
Two Birds	49
The Seer	50
Transvaal 1985	51
The Rising	52
Lear's Ghost to the Audience	53
Karoo Winter	54
Bridge Across the Cole	55

Requiem	56
Strindberg	57
Munich	58
Munich Again	59
Time Lost	60
The Odyssey of Ezra Pound	61
Omen	62
The Villa at Lullingstone	63
The Painter	64
Pablo Picasso	65
Stricken	67
Forgotten Girl	68
The Bahra Road	69
Eyemouth	70
The Road to Damascus	71
Kreuzberg Monastery	72
Prague	73
Homecoming	74
The Old Men	75
Womb of Eve	76
Budapest	77
The Message	78
Paul Cézanne	79
Afterwards	80

Variations

Desolation	83
Many Rivers	84
Adam	85
Conscience at Midnight	86
The Young Orphan	87
De Profundis	88
A Wife's Lament	89
Canzone	90
Spleen	91
Song Without a Name	92
Ballad of the Moon	93
Eiffel Tower	94
War	95

The reader reads the poem
but the poem also reads the reader

Sándor Weöres

Out of the Pool

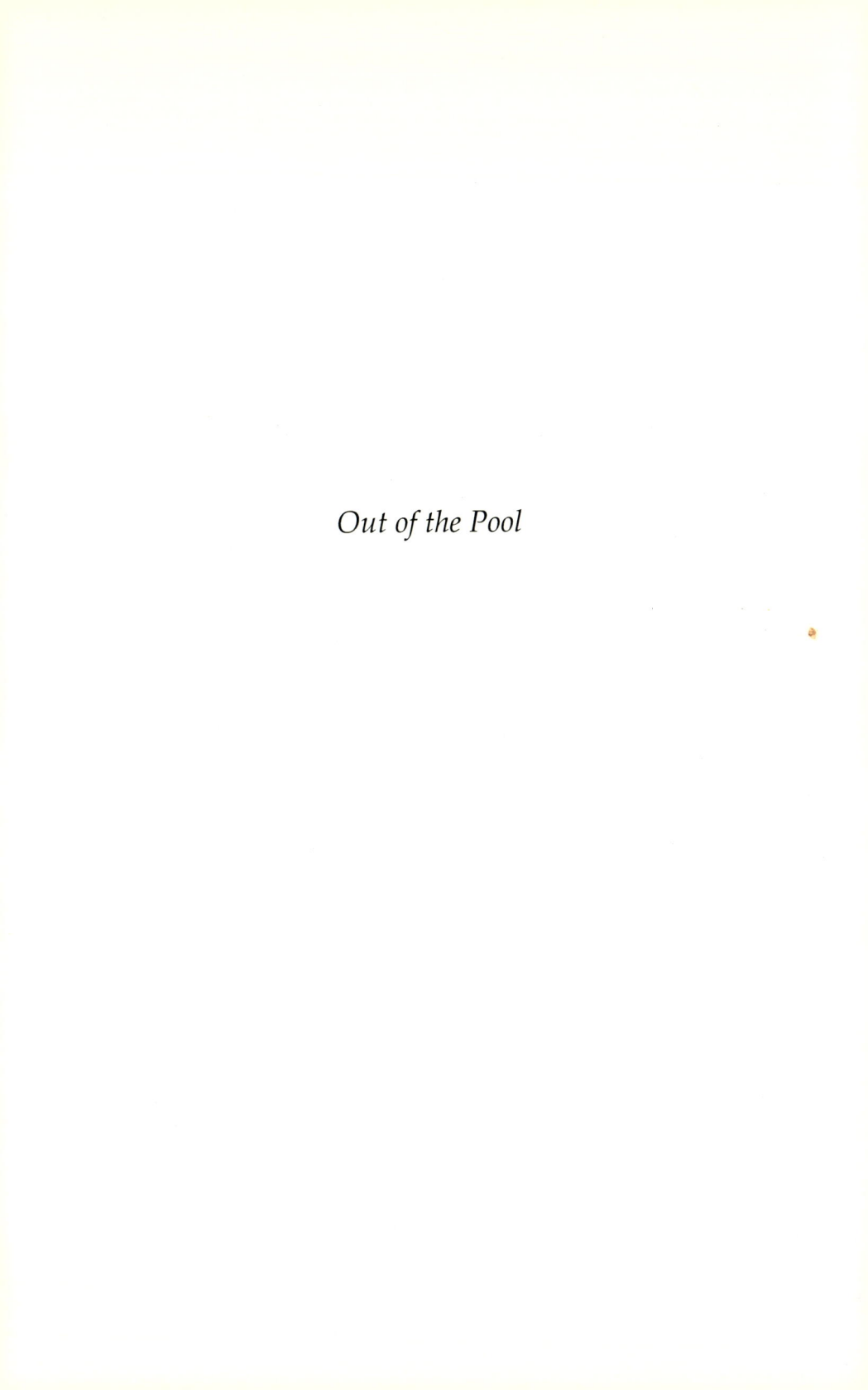

The Kiss
(after Constantin Brancusi)

Far from Rodin's
opulent flexed muscle,
their arms entwining
like possessive snakes,

the two emerging lovers
seek their being
like bubbles rising
to the roof of water,

born out of dogged war
with blade on stone
as words are carved
on paper.

Poor Fisherman
(*after Pierre Puvis de Chavannes*)

The river drags at the land
and will not flow.
All is misty green
except a vapour of sunset
yellowing the horizon.

The fisherman stands
in his barren boat,
faceless and bowed,
empty of promise,
possibly a dream.

Woman and child
are so ethereal
they, too, could be dreams.
Stones spangle the bank
like tarnished coins.

Mostar

This town is ever young,
or so they say,
stone upon cobbled stone,
living off aluminium and wine,
leather and copper work
and the innocent tourist.

We pass the occasional burned-out property,
pick our way past a Mosque under the limes
where urchins pester us to buy their cherries.
Behind it all lie ancient caravans,
the moving shadows of empires
and the strength of water.

The Old Bridge, in Ottoman baroque,
was blasted into history
by a few spiteful shells.
Its gleaming replica
arches the same space
above the limestone-green Neretva

where a man fishing
casts after nature's law, not human folly.
Fear and hatred
still spoor the land,
creviced in those human wounds of war
that never bleed.

Francis Bacon's Pope

*As for the portrait painters, they are
being outdone by the good photographers*
                    Henri Matisse 1942

To outstrip the camera,
distort its reality:
the sitter trapped in violence;

a throned amputee in a
white, sawn-off skirt;
the gilded chair on yellow rockers;

a bespectacled white and purple
see-through apparition
imitating celluloid

flesh and blood
– the sabred nursemaid
on the Odessa Steps –

screaming in dark verticles.

Bus Riders
(after George Segal)

They are not going anywhere;
they are not even going.

Too static to be happening,
their journey never began
and will not end.

Zombie shells of people
on tubular benches,

they never dressed that morning,
they had no morning;
their night won't come.

Nothing will ever happen to them.
They're not like us.

Youth

No moon

and he recalling

starlight in December

her whispers

quickening his yearning

her desire

lost on the night wind

and he crying.

Incomplete

He, being a fool, had howled
the clear call of his nature
from the footlights of the world.
Flesh fell from his bone.

He courted as a ghost
longing to be refleshed,
for the pool of his body
to brim again with blood.

Tears of the incomplete
fall inward where grief burns
in a hidden furnace
and its ashes are blown to words.

Broken Kings

True, their journeys were harsh. All that wandering
over desert, stone and scrub, wilderness lasting
for days without green or water, almost forgetting
the taste of good food and wine. No wonder
the shifty guides bickered and sulked, in the fashion
of their churlish kind, whinging their sullen sorrow.

But there were reasons. You see, it was sorrow
which began it. Caspar, wandering
away from his rich kingdom in a fashion
close to madness, suffering too-long-lasting
grief for his dead Queen, began to wonder
if looking for her like might bring forgetting.

Melchior, on the other hand, was forgetting
nothing. His was a somewhat mundane sorrow:
fleeing a shrewish wife! Well may you wonder
at this once-great King, fallen now to wandering
an alien land in search of a little lasting
peace. She had been too faithful in her fashion.

Now Balthasar, the third one, in the fashion
of Caliphs, had relished power, not forgetting
its partner, wealth, on which he'd set a lasting
worth. So much so that, to his dire sorrow,
he was caught with his hand in the till and so sent wandering,
his bribe for freedom giving cause for wonder.

Three fallen monarchs in their flight – what wonder
brought them together? What event could fashion
in them a single way? Their wandering
had brought no peace, no safety, no forgetting;
they and their hired men grieved in deepening sorrow
and their souls yearned for comfort that was lasting.

The Star that drew them with its ever-lasting
fire paused over a shack! They, in wonder,
dismounted. Was it to this, they asked in sorrow,
their ordeal had brought them? Inside they found a fashion
of poverty without need. Mother, man, not forgetting
the Child, absorbed the star and solved their wandering.

Child, take our greed, our lasting sorrow; fashion
these and our cowardice to gifts; forgetting
all earthly wonder, redeem our wandering.

Sleeping with Icons

Numinous sentinals
guarding their rest;
honeymoon souvenirs
from Budapest.

Seated in dignity,
Virgin and Son
beam golden blessings
from Byzantium.

Doctrine on horseback,
St. George dispatches
red dragon evil;
a lone angel watches.

Holding a Gospel,
one unknown Saint
suffers his martyrdom
without complaint.

Under an absolute
Christ on His throne,
they lie, beatified;
painter unknown.

Peasants Sowing Beans
(after Armand Guillaumin)

Life is tilling soil,
even on golden days,
but here the sweat and pain

seem burned away
by light bursting
from hidden sun

flaring white and
yellow in trees
and glowing over fields.

Yet living muscles
stiffen and backs
ache as this

man and woman
subdue their stubborn earth
in orange fire.

The Seine at Marly
(*after Camille Pissarro*)

The steamer's funnel pants
grey smoke into the air
as the red vessel slants
across the river. Where
the couple stroll, the Seine
bends leftward to the town
where Marly, like a stain,
spreads up the hill and down.

The water chops the light
in segments as it shakes
around the boats. In spite
of the turmoil it makes
and his float's rise and fall,
the angler won't relent;
for him, to fish is all,
to catch irrelevant.

The sky, a bowl of light,
cream flecked with blue, commands
the scene entirely, quite
masters life here, demands
that everything conforms,
as if all things were there
simply to have the forms
and colours that they bear.

Poets – Man and Wife

Each was a mirror

reflecting the other's self.

Lust of a barnyard rooster

holed their dyke,

kicked their one-wedded-flesh

to the back of the shelf.

They liked what they loved

and loved what they didn't like.

Observations

Evening empties the
sky's bowl; morning refills it;
ablutions of time.

Neighbours, armless and
headless, dancing together:
washing blown in wind.

A stirring tangle
of twigs spreads irregular
netting on the sky.

A storm approaches:
the sky forfeits its freedom,
prisoner of clouds.

Thrown by athletic
wind on a wet day: lively
javelins of rain.

Persons

Places

Dreams

D.H.Lawrence

A delicate brat with a sniffy nose
moving about lean Eastwood streets
where gas-lamps bled their yellow light
through the slurried shadow of the mine
and pianos were only a blind groping
for beauty needed more than bread.

Their first meeting, a blaze about him
torching her marriage, a bird in flames
picking about her gravel. The machine
was a failed god, mankind a dying
tree; he and she would each be a door
through which to embrace the universe.

The war-crazed Cornish feared his Frau,
fired both foxes from their lair.
England was killing them. Where now
that rainbow spanning the wilderness?
Peace let them sail, watching their England
sink like a coffin into the sea.

Now he has seeped through that barren landscape
to reach the impulse of all blossom.
Nothing had mattered but the longest journey
to enter as seed into virgin earth,
borne by the love of woman, finding
his way by the blue, forked torch of a flower.

The Guest

I was in love with her;
under their roof
I'd best conceal it.

We climbed the stairs to where
he lay asleep.
Should I reveal it?

I praised her husband's verse.
At once he woke
and with his book

of poems stood there, so
eager to show
me more, his look

of surety a mirror
of my own.
We could define

each other. I knew, were they
and she not his,
both would be mine.

Bavarian Cemetery

Graves loom in the dusk,
lanterns glowing here and there
as if marking the living
from the dead.

Once life used them all;
most breathed years of terror
as naturally as air.

All are earth now,
transitory forms in lasting soil
whether beneath a flame
or unlit grave.

Lanterns serve the living;
candled memories, a hope of life
guttering in the wind.

Renewal

They, side by side,
lay dying, shrunken, bent
and drawn with pain.

I shall destroy worm cried,
mining without relent
from deep disdain.

Joy was denied;
rose petals fell unspent,
seeming in vain

but, as they died,
he broke from her descent
and rose again.

Sir Gawayn's Lament

It was not chastity;
my flesh rose to her flesh
though I did not enter
for an old hag
lay curled like a dog
at the mouth of her body.

I kept the bargain;
every kiss she gave
I gave to him,
receiving in return
his rotting tribute.

She tempted me
to fear for my own harm;
no greater fall than that,
and yet I took it as a charm
to wear in combat!

I sometimes dream
she truly yearned for me
despite her husband's purpose.
I wish to God
I'd loved her thoroughly
and had believed her.

Thomas Hardy

Cast aside as dead at birth
but rescued by an attentive nurse,
he learned early the succour of woman;
a single grain in that year's crop,
one accident in the natural order,
a solitary youth who walked
alone in lasting teenage dreams
of portable romantic love
received by a young lady in brown.

His dream drifted from woman to woman;
each time he sadly woke to see
reality, like morning, harden
upon the wall. Between lay death
untombed, a long lane overhung
with lovelessness as far as the grave.
The gloom of shadows, the draining light,
the fall of darkness made him wish
on many a night no dawn would break.

He lavished his soul on words, saving
nothing for the pain of others, loving
the dead more than the living. Emma
of the white admonishing finger and
hardened mouth, though scarcely cold,
returned as the phantom horsewoman
from enchanting Lyonnesse, haunting
his desolate present, absorbing all
the guilt of his forsaken love.

So he became that grey little man
who could not bear to be touched, who wrote
of an overworld of Spirits that jerked
the puppet strings of man. But still
the systems of the sun rolled on
and any little old song would do
to tell of loss's desolation,
acknowledging both rose and thorn
in each sad, universal cry.

Nightmare

Witch, brooming by,
no gesture or sound
as you whirl around
in your cobalt sky,

I search your stare
to its hollow end
and see you won't care
or ever befriend

me here at the fire
with the scourge to my back,
a spit through my body
and flesh turning black.

Polruan

The coast curves,
dips and crests;
coves nestle the rocks.

Inns clutter
the narrow ways;
crewmen cosset the boats.

Where gulls glide
and caw, tide
opens the harbour claw.

A ferry plies.

My Father
(1894-1932)

You quit your garden
barely into spring,
your seed untended
after just five winters.

I left your pale husk
to its coffin's frame
and blindly reached for you,
despite that absence,

towards your presence
gardening in my veins
through the sixth winter
and beyond.

My Mother
(1891-1975)

Your face,
upon its side,
pillow pale
and still warm,

I kissed farewell
in gratitude
for ended pain
and endless love.

Now your
coffined face,
rouged like
a wax fruit,

copies badly
what you were.
Go quickly and rise
in ending fire.

Sketches from Ireland

Plunge into Dublin's tangle,
flow with its current
which never rests,
drink its heady froth
and dark decay
where night-bridges
stride the Liffey
in a spangle of light.

Spring comes later here;
leaves are still furled
in foetal green;
a soft day in the morning,
gorse hedges glowing Sligo gold,
even in the rain,
and Ben Bulben frowning
on Yeats's dowdy grave.

Houses stand proud
in many-coloured Clifden
where Connemara urges its rock
into the Atlantic
and harbour lanterns lay their pencils
of light upon the water
while Wexford points out to sea,
the Hook lighthouse at its finger-end.

The Other

I am aware
of you, out there
somewhere.

Here joining
seems detached,
and waking

means taking sides,
each forsaking
the other,

locked in
a cell of night,
craving for light.

Frankenheim
(sometime East Germany)

The barbed frontier
rusted into history years ago.
Our car dawdles into Frankenheim,
a small village
near where the wire once ran.

The streets are empty.
Unremarkable lights are coming on
in ordinary windows.
Plain, unromantic houses
grey in the dusk.
All is touchable now,
solid and here,
a child's toy more alluring
seen in a shop window
than held in the hand.

So I shall choose
to remember Frankenheim
seen from the border
eleven years before,
a glimmer of lights beckoning
from a forbidden land,
a gleam of promise whitening
under the same snow.

Two Birds

A sun-blown peacock
planing unrivalled air
on rainbow wings;

a gleam from his eye
had silvered the rock
of the stars.

A bell in the throat
of a wren rings with delight
as he swoops to her side.

Suddenly both are in cages
too strong for their wings.
Lips of the birds through their bars

make a feeble touch
and the wren is drowned
in the peacock's tears.

The Seer

Life was green
yet all around him
grasses lay strawed
in the sun.

The old soothsayer,
gaunt, unwashed and in rags,
was keeping his straw at bay
by seeing visions.

One in particular possessed him.
He gazed at it in wonder,
astonished at its revelation,
amazed at having never known it before.

Transvaal 1985

The country
lay gashed open,
its untended wounds
festering in sun,
the future tightening
around its throat.

On moonless nights
the brooding Milky Way
coiled like a dragon
smouldering on black velvet.

The Rising

Black-robed, the mourners
keep their vigil;
now she is home
and past her peril.

Her bones are ice,
her flesh is snow;
four candles flicker
for our sorrow.

A devil's charm
lured her away;
she has returned
cold as the clay.

At dawn's first gleam
we hear a cry
and, trembling in
strange ecstasy,

she slowly rises
from the bier
and hovers burning
in the air.

Lear's Ghost to the Audience

Perverse madness
to forsake the crown
yet rampage like a king,
spurning honesty
as thankless treason;
suckled on hollow flattery,
trusting in vipers.

Racked by a double storm,
that inner wheel and
the world's wind and rain;
imaged in the mirror
of a naked man
less than a blind man's eyes;
we're beggars beneath ermine.

Treachery and greed,
torture and lechery
seethe in their bilge and breed.
Love, a brief lantern,
led through that rancid mire
straight to a hangman's noose
and left all howling.

Karoo Winter 1992

Vast, open, treeless space;
red earth, ironrock, dust,
roadside fences sieving
tumbleweed from the wind.

In irrigated gardens
grapefruit still balloon on branches
though the Antarctic
frosts the Karoo by dawn.

In squalid shacks or donkey carts
Coloureds are kept
in drink and debt
for ten rand a day.

'Pray for South Africa'
pleads the gentle lady,
fear burning through
the shutters of her eyes.

Bridge Across the Cole
for Roy Holland

After so many years
was it still there
where his bicycle used to speed him
over the brook's unheeding flow,
on towards school?

And now did other boys
still pedal that same route
to – what had it become,
a Comprehensive?

Probably not;
school transport,
parents with cars.
The many change and pass.

Where once the cindered path
sagged at the edges
all was now firmly bricked,
the surface trim,

and one might fancy
its modern, safe façade
shored up a secret:
that same crumbling bridge

with all its memories
brimming in ageing eyes.
On his two sticks
he hobbled to the car.

Requiem

Music at Cambridge: Mozart's Requiem.
His friends from student days,
they would be there
though he would be kept away.

He could see them,
hear them and the music,
but they were unaware
that he was there, yet held away.

The train, perhaps?
But, as he glanced at it,
his elegant watch broke into many pieces
and fell to the ground.

Never to reach the Requiem
though still he heard it,
walking in a land of summer
through avenues of sunlight.

Strindberg

The worm, Strindberg,

coils on the leaf and broods

till the bud emerges,

the bud we naïvely assume

will certainly flower

however the worm intrudes.

Let Strindberg pass

or the bud will never bloom.

Munich

Men surge towards him
through the Underground.
Generations ago, in another place,
they could have been uniformed
with bayonets fixed.

Derricks disfiguring the skyline
where The Church of the Holy Ghost
flaunts its past;
the sanitized tube-trains
always running on time;
the drug-stoned youth
wailing his frenzied harmonica;
the fallow happiness of two last coffees
on the night-lit Maximilianstrasse;

all this is Munich
mindlessly enduring,
like any other city,
a biblical plague in its darkness
and the drip of destruction at noonday.

Munich Again

Twelve years on
and derricks are still
disturbing the sky
with their latticed fingers
set at the same
immaculate angles,
seemingly changeless
amid the change.

Beyond the window
there is no help
for the city enacting
its secret disaster.
Children are always
at play in the park
where trees attend
their permanent meetings
and fledgling swans,
like scudding boats,
test their grey-brown wings
across the lake.

But happiness is now
no longer fallow;
he and she inhabit
a mutual landscape
where fields are tilled
and harvests forever gathered.

Time Lost

We are in time lost
with tempest rising,
fuming of darker gods
havocking at will.

It ends as sudden as it came.
A few wretches stir and rise,
dimly recalling
how it all began

when lush fields liquidized
and the unawares moon
shook where it hung
then plunged into angry water.

They wander dazed
into the desolation,
their burrowing worm a murmur
of the scarce-remembered storm.

The Odyssey of Ezra Pound

Voyaging from his
half-barbaric land,
he found a Europe
gone over the hill;
sailed to dead empires,
dust but for their beauty,
seeking the springs of art,
true civilization,
not in Ithaca or Dublin but
the city of imperishable mind.

Wearied from trying
to heal an ailing culture
and tilting at windmills,
he had no lance for Pisa,
'a dog beneath the hail'.

Fatigue, fatigue; old man,
you cannot rest;
set sail again
and set it down.

Omen

He with his bride
at their wedding. A grim
bird is hiding; their maid
of honour covets him,

scheming behind
her smiles. Beware
the raven in her mind,
matching her hair;

she'll scorn your rings
for carrion. Doom
has dark wings,
naïve bride and groom!

The Villa at Lullingstone

Fertile prize for conquerors
transplanting their sophisticated lives
in northern soil.
They bathe in steamy air,
with slaves to towel and pamper,
wiping the sweat
that beads their bodies clean.

Later to dine with guests
admiring white-and-terracotta mosaic
inched-in beneath their feet,
their host explaining
its mythological theme:
a maiden ravished by a bull
as Virgil tells it.

None of them dreamed
the crude barbarian
would force them back to Rome,
rape their women,
crucify their nuns,
flood up the rivers
to torch their prizes down.

We gaze now on these relics
tracing a Roman finger in the dust.

The Painter

His canvas glowed
with still life,
each fruit
a moon of colour.

The painter vanished,
only to reappear,
began to paint again.
But all had changed.

No colour now was right;
those he could find
would not flow from his brush
to moon on canvas.

Why had it ended?
Others came to stare,
shocked and afraid
at such a death.

Pablo Picasso

The search
does not matter;
finding is all.

Feel an object
with the eye
and form the feeling,
a lie that
tells the truth,
living only
when looked at.

You, the viewer,
cover your nakedness
with what you see.

Africans shaped
their feared spirits
into masks to be
freed from them,
visions and feelings
purged into
multiple forms,

crushing
the eye's
tyranny.

Learn to draw
like a child
and paint
what you know;
there is always
a door waiting
for its key

and only death
can finish
anything.

Stricken

He fell at her entanglements of hair,
pierced by each jutting barb on every strand.
She murmured as he bled upon her there
unloving words he could not understand.

His hands caressed the features of the moon,
fondled each cavity upon its face.
It shook its head and spread a white festoon
of sores out of the flesh his hands embraced.

He bore his stigma bare before the sun,
dancing with stricken joy about the sands.
Then all was still; he stood there quite alone,
the moon's cold leprosy upon his hands.

Forgotten Girl

I do not remember you now;
I remember only our standing
desolately near to each other
while snow drifted helplessly
across the darkening afternoon.

Did you, within your own winter,
dread that virginal disguise
deepening over the desiring earth?

I offered nothing,
feeling numb and asleep beneath you.

And so we stood, motionless and alien,
while snow buried the yearning spring.

The Bahra Road

Man takes
the whole earth
for his own
though sometimes
when it suits him
he's not there

like now
in bleak Bavaria
on a frost-littered track
seeming to lose itself
at the bare
horizon.

An ice-bearing wind
blows unchecked
over dormant fields
ploughed ready
for men to
reclaim

though here
in December's torpor
all is deserted:
untended nature
a wintry Eden
sublime Cézanne emptiness.

Eyemouth

So different now; their children marked the years.
That first time he'd been there to be shown off
to family and friends, long before tears
had blotted marriage lines. He was a 'toff'

to all her crabby relatives, their broad
Berwickshire dialect impenetrable
to unused English ears.
                        Eyemouth had stored
its history in fishing boats and cable-

jumbled quays where auctioneers would gabble
the day's catch away. The old town had
a tangle of narrow alleyways of questionable
mien; down each he'd sensed a Bill Sykes footpad

lurking.

            Her last walk home, the small, lightweight
casket borne first by cousin Robert, the rest
ambling behind. Trim, scrubbed, up-to-date
Council housing lined wide roads in the best

carbolic fashion. The graveyard minister
intoned the ashes to where her parents lay
beneath their headstone.
                        Returning, he saw the sinister
alleyways had gone. Instead were grey

blocks of flats for holidays, a battered
funfair, candyfloss stands, ...*an air that kills*...
the fishing lost. White caravans lay scattered
like a gull's shattered wing across the hills.

The Road to Damascus

His body lay there dying,
its dross falling away,
a kind of empty flying
somewhere. He felt dismay

at lifeless, vacant space.
Dear ones came to grieve
in silence. Then a face
formed above him. Believe

if you will he dreamed. But he,
aware it gazed upon
him with love and absolving pity
that he had denied, was one

with the Lord of Creation who
understood all. Tenderly,
with joy, the face withdrew,
and space returned, empty.

Kreuzberg Monastery

From whirling
blade-sharp snow
warm space receives us.

Ornate opulence
strives to smother
the senses.

No shade to
shelter from glittering
globes and candles.

Kneeling figures
make worship's
concurring gesture.

It is a way,
but not
the only way.

Prague

The city sprawls beyond the river,
its terracotta rooftops strewn on hills;
jagged spires claw the sky;
Skodas harass the streets,
roaring full-throttle on the road to Brno.

A cake thinly-iced with its own history
of Gothic vaulted roof and the sung Mass,
a sunburst chorus of stained glass
and Alphonse Mucha's arabesques of light,
his peasant woman frozen to the landscape.

Dark lies beneath: drunks quarrel in tramcars,
high-rise suburbs spawn their empty reaches
of anonymous lives where the city breaks its heart,
the archetypal city.

Homecoming

He was archer and arrow maker;
apprentices studied his skills.
Their shafts completed,
he'd tried to show
how to hit a distant tree

but his arrow had fallen short.
As he went forward to seek it
he found himself
walking once more
among glades of forgotten childhood.

Nearby, boys were calling
There it is, Billesley!
He saw his arrow
beyond a stream
and knew that they had named him

after the place he'd come from
so many years before,
glad that they
had accepted him,
joyful to be home.

The Old Men

In Ward Sixteen the old men gather
like shattered pigeons downed from flight.
Some know it's over; some would rather
dream their past life of wings despite

no hope of take-off. Now their sky
has shrunk to bed-pans, drips and care;
boredom is standard, leavened by
the nurses' optimistic flair.

The smallness of it all still grows
unalterably smaller – why
they do not know. A window shows
vast life, eternity and sky.

Womb of Eve

He comes to her
as a child nearing the edge
of a primeval forest.

Leaves glowing in sunlight
beckon to him above
unapproachable darkness.

Mystified and afraid, he is
drawn through the gladdening leaves
down into the dark

to be lost and blind
deep in the womb of Eve
and beyond the world.

Budapest

Fought over by forgotten thousands,
their corpses rotted into monuments,
Heroes Square lies paved over blood.

A motor vessel chugs along the Danube,
discharging trippers at occasional islands,
bearing others north towards Visegrad.

Returning, the sliding river darkens,
rippling with silver as the city approaches,
gleaming with its own stars.

Beneath some ancient steps
an ageing couple argue wearily,
their quarrel old and hopeless as themselves.

Elsewhere the lovers lie,
murmuring over and over
blithe promises of always and forever.

The Message

The ghostly vehicle lurched on;
its passengers were seated tight
and I among them, driven far
through the bleak night

on a cold, nameless journey. Each
stared at the others silently;
then one in martyr's black arose
and spoke to me.

At once each hostile gaze was fixed
upon us. He just looked me through
and said: Tell them I did not die;
I'm coming too.

I turned and saw that we were all
now in a vast Cathedral, crammed
as earlier to the doors. Were we
the blest or damned?

I spoke but could not hear my voice.
The saving message I had striven
in vain to tell them failed. I would
not be forgiven.

Paul Cézanne

He strove to see the world
without a memory,
paring nature to its anatomy
and then refleshing it
to perfect form
in which his feeling lingers
like a fragrance.

His colours make images
that have felt rain
and seen the sun rise,
looking as the blind
would feel them,
his gardener in cool flames
from a fragmenting sun.

A master in chains
to the innocent
thoughts of his eyes,
in his landscapes every
instrument is playing,
Edens without mankind,
the occasional road empty.

Afterwards

Rising
at time's ending,
the astonished moon sliding
over the edge of the sea.

Coming in
transfigured
with eyes all-seeing.

Rising
with hair wind-streaming
and new blood pulsing.

Coming in
renewed beginning
with spine re-stretching,
shaking away the coffin's dust.

Variations

Desolation
(after Georg Trakl)

The castle's fanged and ragged towers
brood on the lake. All wild birds fear
its rotted groves. Rank fungus sours
the dank and fetid air. It's here

the past has died. A sad review
of fevered nights and kisses flows
around the walls, corrupts into
a petrified, distorted rose.

Swans glide between dense reeds and palid
lilies in whose water stands
a ruined tree. From there rise squalid
shades like severed female hands.

He sits in one decaying room,
looks on his desolation from
a cobwebbed window, one vast tomb
of sadness reaching far and on.

Many Rivers
(*after the Katha Upanishad*)

The path of earthly pleasure
leads to the river of sorrows
where we wither like famished corn.

Treading life's gruelling road
we do not know
the darkness of our ignorance.

Bodily senses falter;
do not lament for that
which ebbs away.

Many rivers flow from the heart;
only the shining stream
carries one upward.

Adam
(after Frederico Garcia Lorca)

Blood wets the dawn without a sound
amid the woman's new-birth groans.
The window bears the print of bones;
her voice leaves crystals in the wound.

Firmly the light breaks in, a foil
of white edging the mystery fable,
bringing the cooling scent of apple
rushing from her veins' turmoil.

Adam, in fever and alone,
dreams of an infant neophyte,
mounted and nearing, cheeks full-blown.

A second Adam, recondite,
lies on a seedless moon of stone,
dreaming a coming child of light.

Conscience at Midnight
(after Charles Baudelaire)

As it strikes midnight, let the clock
ironically judge our deeds
throughout this day which now recedes
into our memory, take stock
of our ridiculous pose. The trick
is, somehow we should recognize
that what we did was just a guise,
like when we played the heretic

blaspheming against Christ, that rare,
least-questionable god. It's like
acting how some obnoxious tyke
sucks up to a fat millionaire
who's worth only the goriest
fate in hell. What do we prove
by desecrating all we love
and praising all that we detest?

Just like a servile torturer,
we heaped scorn on a helpless man
reviled by others. Then we ran
to laud stupidity. We err
in kissing mindless matter, pray
avidly to it. We'd not guessed
our crass subservience as we blessed
the sickly radiance of decay.

Finally, as if we could
reduce mind's vortex to a daze,
we priests of language should give praise
to rapture of sad themes. We stood,
however, in a different place,
drank without thirst and over-ate
without hunger. Obliterate
that light so darkness hides our face!

The Young Orphan
(after an anonymous Chinese poem 25-220AD)

To be an orphan
is truly bitter.
My tears fall like rain.

When I had parents
I rode in a carriage
with four noble horses.

Now I must work hard
with no winter coat
nor sandals to tread the frost.

Look how my hands are chapped,
my head full of lice
and my face grimed by labour.

I long to be dead
and join my father and mother
in Yellow Springs under the earth.

To be an orphan
is truly bitter.
My tears fall like rain.

De Profundis
(*after Georg Trakl*)

Black rain falls on the stubble-field
where a gaunt tree stands alone.
Wind stirring through vacant huts
brings the evening's sorrowful moan.

An orphan-girl picks the last few ears
of corn, bright-eyed in the gloom
of twilight, her womb passively waiting
for the heavenly bridegroom.

Homeward shepherds found a body
rotted in a thorn-bush.
Far from its village a shadow drinks
earth's silence from the spring's flush.

Cold metal clasps my brow as spiders
search for my heart. A gust
blows out the light in my mouth. I grow stiff
with the waste of stardust.

A Wife's Lament
(after an anonymous Anglo-Saxon poem in the Exeter Book)

My louring lord left me for the sea's lure,
braving the burying waves to be broken from me,
leaving me lonely, lamenting my loveless life,
wishing I knew of his wandering, weary and worn.

His people had plotted and planned to part us forever,
and one whom I felt was a friend proved faithless and false
and put it about I was partial to passing trade,
driving my dear one to dice for his doom with the sea.

They were loathsome lies. We loved as no others had loved.
Now I have fled from the falsehood to fend in the forest
barbed with briars, through hamlets hollow with hate.
Woe withers one who lives wandering, longing for love.

Canzone
(after Sonnet 35 by Francesco Petrarca)

Alone, with heavy tread, I walk wasteland
where no-one comes. Weighed down by misery
yet sharp-eyed as a hawk, I'm watchfully
afraid of finding footprints in the sand.

I have no mask, can't hide behind my hand
the shame of my distress. All eyes would see
my joy has become sorrow. They would be
the wind with which my inward fire is fanned.

I think it likely that all mountains, plains –
the whole of nature – knows what I endure
which I so avidly conceal from men.

And yet I can't believe that Love disdains
to pity me once more, however poor
my state. Surely he'll come to me again?

Spleen
(after Charles Baudelaire)

When the low, leaden sky weighs like a lid
on the groaning mind, tortured by endless strain,
and pours from the whole horizon its intrepid
darkness, day sadder than night's worst bane;

when earth is no more than a dripping prison cell
in which hope reels like a bat bruising its wing
on the treacherous, slimy walls, a confining hell,
and beating its crazed head on the rotted ceiling;

when streaks of rain form into window-grilles
in some gigantic prison where despair reigns
and a silent horde of loathsome spiders spills
its way in, weaving webs inside our brains;

then, suddenly, bells swing with rage and hurl
their venom to the sky, for all the world
like frenzied banshees in a deadly skirl
of endless wailing for their underworld,

and a trail of mourners and their hearse careers,
with neither drums nor music, through my soul
and hope, in its defeat, bursts into tears
while grief, deep in my skull, thrusts her black flagpole.

Song Without a Name
(*after an anonymous German lyric, date unknown*)

Last night as I lay sleeping,
a nightmare came to me:
there grew within my garden
a tree of rosemary.

My garden was a churchyard,
each bed of flowers a tomb
and falling to the flowerbeds
was every leaf and bloom.

I took a golden vessel
to catch the falling dead;
it slipped and shattered; from it
ran pearls of rosy red.

I fear those pearls, my darling;
come, hurry to my side.
What is their crimson meaning?
My loved one – have you died?

Ballad of the Moon
(after Frederico Garcia Lorca)

The moon, in her hooped petticoat,
comes to the forge.
The child looks and looks.

'Moon, moon, run away!
If the gypsies come they will make
a white necklace from your heart.'

'Child, let me dance;
when the gypsies come they will find
your head on the anvil.'

'Moon, moon, run away!
I can hear the horsemen coming,
drumming the plain.'

Inside the forge
the child's eyes are closing,
the bronze gypsies are coming.

The owl hoots
and the moon flies through the sky
leading the child by the hand.

Inside the forge
The breeze is watching, watching,
the gypsies are weeping.

Eiffel Tower
(*after Guillaume Apollinaire*)

You are weary of the old world,
Eiffel Tower,
shepherding your flock of bridges;

you have turned your back
on ancient Greece and Rome;

in the Paris you bestride,
even the cars seem ancient.

But religion has somehow
managed to stay brand-new,
simple as airfield hangars;

God dies on Friday,
rises again on Sunday
and Christ climbs the sky
better than any pilot.

He well understands
His twenty centuries
and the twentieth
has now become a bird
climbing like Jesus
skyward.

War
(after Georg Trakl)

This autumn evening the woods ring
with weapons. The sun strolls over blue
lakes and golden plains. There sing
the broken mouths of the dying who

lie under red clouds, troops
who feel the angry arms of the night
folding about them. A fierce god stoops
to gaze on their black decay. In spite

of carnage, Sister's shadow struts
through the avenue of blood to the grim
jig of battle. The unborn corrupts.
Those with a son should cherish him.